情人节

**Customs, Traditions and Landmarks |
Non-Fiction Series**

Copyright © 2022 by Level Learning, INC. and Washington Yu Ying PCS™
Original and Edited Text Copyright © 2022 by Washington Yu Ying PCS™

All rights reserved. No part of this book in whole or part may be reproduced without written permission from the publisher.

Published by Level Learning, INC.
Content Contributors:
Washington Yu Ying PCS™
Level Learning - Jingyao Qi

Illustrations by: Matt Austin

Leveling classification based on Level Learning standard.
For full description, visit www.levellearning.com

ISBN 978-1-64040-020-7
Simplified Chinese Edition

About Level Learning:

Level Learning provides a literacy focused curriculum specifically designed for K-12 Chinese as a Second Language classrooms. Our program offers 20 levels of specific and detailed objectives, leveled texts and passages, mastery-based online assessment, and analytics to enable data-driven instruction. Level Learning reading curriculum for both literature and informational text emphasize grammar and comprehension skills to help teachers develop confident and independent Chinese language readers. The non-fiction series of books are specifically designed to support our informational text course based on multiple national standards. To learn more about our entire offering, visit www.levellearning.com.

About Washington Yu Ying PCS™:

Washington Yu Ying PCS is a Mandarin English dual language immersion International Baccalaureate (IB) World school. Yu Ying's mission is to inspire and prepare young people to create a better world by challenging them to reach their full potential in a nurturing Chinese/English educational environment. Yu Ying's comprehensive IB, dual immersion curriculum equips students with global competencies for success in the real world. As a leader in immersion education, Yu Ying is determined to advance Chinese language programs and global citizenry education by helping other schools create and strengthen their Chinese programs. For more information, email: products@washingtonyuying.org

二月						
星期一	星期二	星期三	星期四	星期五	星期六	星期日
1	2	3	4	5	6	
7	8	9	10	11	12	13
(14)	15	16	17	18	19	20
21	22	23	24	25	26	27
28						

每年的2月14日是情人节。情人节是西方国家的一个传统节日,也是大家向自己喜欢的人表达心意的节日。

情人节不是只有爱人之间才可以庆祝的节日。在西方国家,情人节是所有的人都可以庆祝的节日。

在情人节这一天，人们可以**送礼物**给家人、同学、老师、朋友、**同事，或者**其他喜欢的人。

情人节的礼物通常是卡片、花、糖果等。也有很多人喜欢自己亲手做礼物。

很多学校都有一些情人节的**活动**，比如亲手做卡片或**手工艺品**等。小朋友可以把做好的礼物送给他们喜欢的人。

情人节已经有很多年的**历史**了。现在，越来越多的人庆祝情人节。

你会庆祝情人节吗?怎么庆祝呢?

Glossary

	Pinyin	English Definition
情人节	qíng rén jié	Valentine's Day
传统	chuán tǒng	tradition
节日	jié rì	festival
表达	biǎo dá	to express
心意	xīn yì	feeling, emotion
爱人	ài rén	lovers
庆祝	qìng zhù	celebrate
所有	suǒ yǒu	all
送	sòng	to give
礼物	lǐ wù	gifts
同事	tóng shì	coworkers, colleague
或者	huò zhě	or
通常	tōng cháng	usually
卡片	kǎ piàn	greeting card
活动	huó dòng	activities

	Pinyin	English Definition
手工艺品	shǒu gōng yì pǐn	handmade crafts
历史	lì shǐ	history

www.ingramcontent.com/pod-product-compliance
Lightning Source LLC
Chambersburg PA
CBHW041225070526
44584CB00001B/108